Did you know...
If you read carefully you could find two small
incorrect facts in this book. As you read,
see if you can discover our bloopers!

Here are two hints:
The Wright brothers first flew in 1903.
Turtles are amphibious reptiles.

For more information on the Wright brothers
and amphibians log onto:
www.gentlegiraffe.com and click on Books.

Cherry Blossom Friends

Words and Pictures by
Corkey Hay DeSimone

Cherry Blossom Friends

A suggestion on how to read this book.

This is a book about the incredible gift of the cherry blossoms, and all the wonderful animals that live around the blossoming trees in Washington, D.C. As you will see, it is designed to be read to a wide range of listeners. Each page has two distinct sections; the "Rhyme and Riddle" and the "Did you know...". It is suggested to first read the "Rhyme and Riddle" section from cover to cover. You can then read the "Did you know..." sections which do not need to be read in sequence. They are just interesting facts that add to the experience of the cherry blossoms.

Have you heard about the 3,000
famous flowering trees,
that blossom each spring
in the Washington breeze?

Given as a gift to Washington, D.C.
from the city of Tokyo, Japan.
Yes, the Americans and Japanese
had a plan.

To plant these pretty pink trees all in a row,
as a reminder that friendship
can blossom and grow.

Can you guess what trees they can be?
Turn the page and you will see.

The Japanese Cherry Trees

Each Spring, a lantern is lit,
and the flame burns bright.
Many people whisper
"What a beautiful sight".

It sits beside the Tidal Basin,
among the cherry trees.
It was gift of friendship
from the Japanese.

What special lantern could this be?
Turn the page and you will see.

Did you know...
In 1912, the same year that the Wright brothers first flew and the
Titanic sank, 3,000 cherry trees were given as a gift from one
capital city to another -- Tokyo, Japan, to Washington, D.C.
How did they get 3,000 trees from Tokyo to Washington?
First, they crossed the Pacific Ocean on a steamship.
They arrived in port on the west coast of America, but still had a
long way to go. Next, they were carefully placed in a
cooled freight train, which crossed 2,500 miles
from the west coast to the east coast.
The journey took 40 days.
Wow, what a trip!

The Japanese Stone Lantern

Gifts of friendship are not the only thing,
that you can see each year in the spring.

These beautiful blossoming cherry trees
are a home to the butterflies, birds and bees.
A place for raccoons to climb and foxes to hide,
for squirrels to run, jump and glide,
for blue herons to perch and robins to nest,
for skunks to sleep or take a rest,
for turtles to sun on a log sunken halfway,
for bald eagles to soar, swoop and play.

Many animals enjoy the gift of trees from Japan.
Turn the page and name as many animals as you can.

Did you know...
The Stone Lantern that sits beside the Tidal Basin is over 350 years old
and has a twin in Japan! The lantern has not always sat surrounded by cherry
trees in Washington, D.C. It once stood outside an ancient temple in Japan,
where its twin lantern still stands to this day. In 1954, Japan presented the Stone
Lantern to America, a gift celebrating 100 years of friendship. Sadly, it was not 100
years of perfect peace. In 1941, Japan and America went to war. After four years
the war came to an end, and it was time to mend their friendship.
The Stone Lantern is an important symbol of renewed friendship and peace.
It is lit every spring in a ceremony during the
National Cherry Blossom Festival.

Are you ready? Listen please,
for your first riddle about animals
that live around the cherry trees.

I nest in the cherry blossoms
of Washington, D.C.
I am a small bird,
can you find me?

Just like the cherry blossoms,
I am a sign of spring.
I sit in the cherry trees
and sing, sing, sing.

I have dark gray wings
and an orange chest.
I lay blue eggs in my nest.

Take a guess, what can I be?
Turn the page and you will see!

Robin

I swim under the cherry blossoms
of Washington, D.C.
I am an amphibian,
can you find me?

I live in water, but lay eggs on land,
I dig my nest in soft soil and sand.
On the Potomac River is where I dwell.
I have a long neck and a protective shell.

Take a guess, what can I be?
Turn the page and you will see.

Did you know...
The Washington Monument is the tallest building in
Washington, D.C. It took 36 years to build. During the Civil War
its construction had to stop because the builders ran out of money.
For 27 years the Washington Monument stood less than one-third
finished in the middle of the National Mall. It was only 156 feet tall.
When completed in 1884, it stood 555 feet tall
and it was the tallest building in the world. Four years later the
Eiffel Tower in Paris, France stole the title. You can easily see
the Washington Monument rising above the cherry blossoms.

Turtle

I climb in the cherry blossoms
of Washington, D.C.
I come out at night,
can you find me?

In the spring I can have
six babies, but usually three.
I can make my den in a hollow tree.
I have a masked face and a ringed tail.
Watch for me and my babies on the trail.

Take a guess, what can I be?
Turn the page and you will see.

Did you know...
The Japanese cherry trees were planted before the Jefferson Memorial
was built. Many people were not happy because some cherry trees were to
be moved to make room for the new monument. A group of women promised
to chain themselves to the trees, so the trees would not be cut down.
A deal was made and it was promised that new trees would be planted to
replace any lost trees. Today, it is hard to imagine the cherry blossoms
without the Jefferson Memorial.
Thomas Jefferson was our third president and a great
and smart man, who wanted a country that was free,
where everyone could learn and enjoy liberty.

Raccoon

I soar above the cherry blossoms
of Washington, D.C.
I'm a symbol of
America and liberty.
I'm a bird of prey,
can you find me?

I have bright yellow eyes,
talons and a hooked beak.
I have a white feathered head
and my call is a shriek.

Take a guess, what can I be?
Turn the page and you will see.

Did you know...
From 1776 to 1791, the government of the United States had no capital
and met in seven different cities. George Washington helped pick the site
of the new capital city that was later named after him. He laid the
U.S. Capitol Building cornerstone and since then the building has changed
and grown. During the War of 1812, the British set the building ablaze. If not
for heavy rains, the fire might have burned for days. When the war came to an
end the capitol building was rebuilt. A hundred years later the Japanese
cherry trees were planted on the grounds. If only George Washington could
see how beautiful his capitol grounds would be, painted in pink and green
during the blossoming of the cherry trees!

Bald Eagle

I fish beneath the cherry blossoms
of Washington, D.C.
I'm a large wading bird,
can you find me?

I have a long neck and up to a 6 foot wing span.
I love to eat small fish whenever I can.
On my long legs, I hunt, by standing still in one place.
I fly along the Tidal Basin with incredible grace.

Take a guess, what can I be?
Turn the page and you will see.

Did you know...
In 1782, the founding fathers made the American Bald Eagle the symbol of
the United States. Almost 200 years later, the bald eagle almost
became extinct. Hunting and the use of a pesticide which thinned the shells of
the eagles' eggs were at fault. Since the eagles were not able to lay healthy
eggs, they had very few chicks. The bald eagle was
declared an endangered species, eagle hunting was outlawed and the use of
the pesticide was stopped. The American Bald Eagle bounced back!
Now you can see bald eagles flying over the cherry blossoms of D.C.
and along the Potomac River, healthy and free.

Blue Heron

I hide among the cherry blossoms
of Washington, D.C.
I'm smart and sly,
can you find me?

I am part of the dog family, but not a pet.
I'm a wild animal, but not a threat.
I have black-tipped ears
and a long bushy tail.
You can spot my furry
red coat without fail.

Take a guess, what can I be?
Turn the page and you will see.

Did you know...
In 1914, two years after the cherry trees arrived, the first stone of the
Lincoln Memorial was set. There are 36 columns around the outside of the Lincoln
Memorial, one for each state that belonged to the Union the year Lincoln died.
The names of the 48 lower states are carved on the band above the columns. If
your eyesight is very good you might find your state! If you are from Alaska or
Hawaii, these states were added later and markers can be found inside the memorial.
Also inside is the statue of Lincoln sitting deep in thought. He is 19 feet tall and
weighs 350,000 pounds. President Lincoln was our sixteenth president.
He freed the slaves and held the country together.
Yes, Lincoln was a man of courage and one of the greats!

Red Fox

I live among the cherry blossoms
of Washington, D.C.
I'm black and white, can you find me?

You can smell me coming a mile away.
Don't get too close or else I'll spray!

Take a guess, what can I be?
Turn the page and you will see.

Did you know...
The Smithsonian Castle is the oldest building on the National Mall.
How it came to be is an amazing story. James Smithson was from England and had
never ever come to America, but when he died in 1829, he gave his life savings to the
United States of America. His fortune was sent to the USA in 11 boxes
containing gold coins. They were melted down and made into American gold coins
and were worth over $500,000.00. He had asked that the money be used to set up
the Smithsonian where people could share all the things that they learned and
discovered. Now there are nineteen museums, and 9 research sites.
His gift grows and blossoms just as the cherry trees do.

Skunk

I can graze among the cherry blossoms
of Washington, D.C.
I find cherry leaves tasty,
can you find me?

My father is a buck and my mother is a doe.
I walk on hooves, I have no toes.
My tail has a white underside which I flash when alarmed,
if I think I might be chased, hunted or harmed.

Take a guess, what can I be?
Turn the page and you will see.

Did you know...
The White House is where the American President works and lives,
but it was never George Washington's office or home. It was built in 1800 of
sandstone, and in the War of 1812, the British set it on fire.
Some people say that it was first painted white to cover the burn marks.
Others say the white paint helps protect the sandstone from cracking in the wet and
cold winters. Those are some of the stories about why it is white. What we do know is
that when First Lady Helen Taft lived in the White House, she played a major part
in getting the Japanese cherry trees planted around the Tidal Basin.
She personally helped plant the first two cherry trees.
Those two trees are still alive today and sit at the edge of the
Tidal Basin with historic markers at their base.

Whitetail Deer

I climb among the Cherry
Blossoms of Washington, D.C.
I love acorns, can you find me?

I run up the trunks
and scurry around the trees.
I leap from branch to branch
with incredible ease.

Take a guess, what can I be?
Turn the page and you will see.

Did you know...
In 1958, the Japanese Pagoda that sits by the Tidal Basin was
another generous gift from Japan. Like a puzzle, it arrived in many
pieces, without building instructions. Many people helped put it
together. It came in five big crates and weighed 3,800 pounds.
It is made of stone.
In Japan, to show the balance of nature, gardens include water,
stone and plants. The Japanese stone Pagoda sits beneath the
cherry trees, at the side of the Tidal Basin,
perfectly mixing all three elements in harmony.

Gray Squirrel

I buzz around the cherry blossoms
of Washington, D.C.
I'm an important insect, can you find me?

One of my jobs is to pollinate plants.
Other plant pollinators include
butterflies, beetles and ants.
I sip and gather nectar from flower to flower.
With it, I can make honey and it gives me power.

Take a guess, what can I be?
Turn the page and you will see.

Did you know...
The Smithsonian Carousel that twirls and whirls around has 57 carved
wooden jumping horses, one menagerie animal, two chariots,
one spinning tub and one special dragon. It was originally built in 1947
by the famous carousel maker, The Allan Herschell Company.
They made more than 3,000 carousels, many of which were used by traveling carnivals.
The Smithsonian Carousel was first in a park in Baltimore before it was moved
to the National Mall in 1975. You can ride this carousel every day but Christmas
day. The carousel is close to the Smithsonian Castle on the National Mall.
After you take a ride you can walk through the blossoming cherry trees
in the Castle garden outside.

Bees

I stroll among the cherry blossoms
of Washington, D.C.
I love to picnic, can you find me?

I'm the only animal that can plant a tree,
and save land for wildlife to roam free.

Take a guess, what can I be?
Turn the page and you will see.

Did you know...
In 1965, The Japanese gave Washington 3,800 more trees.
Some of the originals had been lost to cold winters and disease.
When you receive a gift it is important to give in return
and in 1982 it was America's turn. A flood destroyed the Yoshino
cherry trees in Japan. The Japanese horticulturalists came with a plan.
They took cuttings from the Washington cherry trees
so they could replace the trees that were lost.

You and me!

Did the Japanese and Americans foresee,
all the good things that come with a tree?
Like all the animals that frolic, eat and live,
and the fresh clean air that the trees give.

There is no better gift that you can give,
to the earth, your city or the place you live.
So plant at least one tree each and every spring,
and prepare to be amazed by the gifts it will bring.

Did you know...
The flowering cherry trees are planted all over the city.
It is estimated that about 3,700 cherry trees are still growing in Washington, D.C.
Over 6,800 trees have been thoughtfully given to Washington by Japan.
The cherry trees remind us of the great friendship between America and Japan,
and that all friendships need attention and care. We must not take friendship for
granted. We must share, be fair, and always remember that good,
strong friendships are extremely rare.

About the Author and Illustrator

Corkey Hay DeSimone lives with her
family close to Washington, D.C.
She was the founding owner, designer and
illustrator for Corkey's Kids,
a children's clothing company.
In 2003, after 13 years,
she sold Corkey's Kids so that she could
turn her focus to writing and illustrating
educational children's books.

After selling Corkey's Kids,
she renamed her company
Gentle Giraffe Press.
She has since written, illustrated
and published 22 books
and several more are in the works.

Books By
Corkey Hay DeSimone

The Planet Hue

Mammal Animal Board Book
First Edition
Mammal Animal Activity Book
First Edition

Air and Space Board Book
Air and Space Activity Book

Sports Legends Board Book
Sports Legends Activity Book

Panda Promise Hardbound Book
Panda Promise Board Book
Panda Promise Activity Book

Dinosaur Explore Board Book
Dinosaur Explore Activity Book

Mammal Animal Board Book
Second Edition
Mammal Animal Activity Book
Second Edition

Desert Dwellers Board Book
Desert Dwellers Activity Book
Desert Crawlers Board Book
Desert Crawlers Activity Book

Butterfly Friends Hardbound Book
Butterfly Friends Board Book
Butterfly Friends Coloring Book